WHAT IS A HORSE?

Ron Hirschi

photographs by

Linda Quartman Younker and Ron Hirschi

Walker and Company
New York

Kristen!
HAPPY TRAILS!

For my mom and dad.   L.Q.Y.

First published in the United States of America in 1989
by Walker Publishing Company, Inc.

Published simultaneously in Canada by Thomas Allen & Son
Canada, Limited, Markham, Ontario

Library of Congress Cataloging-in-Publication Data

Hirschi, Ron.
What is a horse? / Ron Hirschi ; photographs by Linda Younker.
p.   cm.
Summary: Brief text and photographs present various types of
horses engaged in such activities as rodeos, racing, nuzzling, and
running free.
ISBN 0-8027-6876-8.—ISBN 0-8027-6877-6 (lib. bdg.)
1. Horses—Juvenile literature. [1. Horses.] I. Younker, Linda,
ill. II. Title.
SF302.H57 1989 88-37524
636.1—dc19 CIP AC

Printed in Hong Kong

10 9 8 7 6 5 4 3 2 1

Book design by Laurie McBarnette

WHAT
IS A
HORSE?

A horse is a friend waiting
by the corner gate.

Horses are saddles, bridles,
stirrups, and boots.

They are pintos and
appaloosas.

They are the swish of a tail
and the smell of sweet hay.

A horse is a rodeo ride and
a dusty cattle drive.

Horses prance, jump, nuzzle,
and tease.

They pull carriages,
play polo games,

patrol city streets, and fly fast
as the wind around a track.

They need plenty of food,
clean water,

a warm place to rest, and love.

Horses have mothers, fathers,
and friends.

Horses are wild.

Horses are free,

even when they
belong to you.

AFTERWORD

Horses are wonderful companions. They are also obligations, needing much attention and care. Like other social animals, horses must associate with others of their kind. They enjoy our gentle hands and respond to our voices.

Horses seem to demand the same kinds of attention and affection we demand from our friends and family. Maybe that is why young people are so attracted to horses.

Because of the great demands they place on their owner, horses can help a young person learn the true meaning of responsibility and what it means to care for another. All the basic needs for food, shelter, water, and warmth must be attended to. These are essentials. Additional love nourishes and enriches both horse and owner. Then they can ride together as one.

May we all be so lucky to ride beneath an endless western sky.